This journal belongs to

_____

Introduction

Animals are symbolic of the earthly embodiment of human traits and behaviour. We sometimes seek to deny that we are animals, but when we are driven by instinct and biological imperatives, our animalistic urges often become apparent. This is not necessarily a bad thing.

Animals are naturally intuitive, possess an inherent understanding of the world around them, and use all of their senses to experience life. They do not burden themselves with unhealthy emotions and restrictive dogma. This allows them to live in a very natural and flowing manner, in harmony with their environment. They are the perfect guides to teach you how to do the same.

Our animal guides can also teach us to honour the flow of natural cycles and seasons. There is a natural beginning and ending to all things. They will teach you to see that when something – a moment or an experience – comes to an end, there is always a new opportunity or moment waiting to manifest.

Your animal guides will teach you to honour the ebb and flow of life. Speak to them. Share your confidences with them.

Trust …

… and then take a moment to go back and reread what you have written in the preceding weeks and months. What stands out? What thoughts and feelings arise when you read about your past experiences? Is there a recurrent theme? Many animals are territorial. They will travel using familiar pathways because they know those pathways will lead them to where they need to be. Regular use of a journal, and looking back on the written history it contains, will also allow you to recognise the pathways that take you to where you need or want to be.

Let your senses, instincts, and intuition be your guides, and travel well.

Blessings and love,

Ravynne